Apples
and
Pomegranates

A Family Seder for Rosh Hashanah

Rahel Musleah

illustrations by Judy Jarrett

KAR-BEN
PUBLISHING

For my family, who makes every new year joyous.

–R.M.

To my mother, Mary, who didn't quite make it for the publication; and for my granddaughter, Claire, who will love seeing Apples and Pomegranates!

–J.J.

Key to Transliteration
(Based on the Jewish Publication Society Style Sheet)

a: as in farm	*ai:* as in eye
e: as in fed	*tz:* as in rabbits
o: as in hope	*h (het):* as in Bach
i: as in hit or street	*h (hay):* as in hello
u: as in flute	*kh:* as in Bach
ei: as in hay	

Text copyright © 2004 by Rahel Musleah
Illustrations copyright © 2004 by Judy Jarrett

Kar-Ben Publishing
A division of Lerner Publishing Group, Inc.
241 First Avenue North
Minneapolis, Minnesota 55401 U.S.A.
800-4KARBEN

Website address: www.karben.com

Library of Congress Cataloging-in-Publication Data

Musleah, Rahel.
    Apples and pomegranates : a Rosh Hashanah seder / by Rahel Musleah ; illustrations by Judy Jarrett.
        p.   cm.
    Text in English, prayers in English and Hebrew.
    ISBN: 978-1-58013-123-0 (pbk. : alk. paper)
    1. Rosh ha-Shanah seder—Juvenile literature. 2. Judaism—Sephardic rite—Prayer-books and devotions—Juvenile literature. 3. Judaism—Liturgy—Texts—Juvenile literature. 4. Food—Religious aspects—Judaism—Juvenile literature. [1. Rosh ha-Shanah. 2. Judaism—Customs and practices. 3. Prayer-books and devotions. 4. Seder. 5. Holidays. 6. Food—Religious aspects. 7. Hebrew language materials—Bilingual.] I. Jarrett, Judy, ill. II. Title.
BM695.N5M87 2004
296.4'5315—dc22   2003026461

Manufactured in the United States of America
3 — DP — 2/1/11

Contents

Introduction

A seder for Rosh Hashanah? Isn't a seder supposed to be for Passover? Would you eat matzah on Hanukkah or build a sukkah for Purim?

The Rosh Hashanah seder is actually a very old custom, dating back 2000 years. In the Talmud (*Horayot 12a*), Rabbi Abaye suggests that at the beginning of each new year, people should eat the following foods that grow abundantly and so symbolize prosperity: pumpkin, rubia (a bean-like vegetable), leeks, beets, and dates. Jewish communities throughout the world—especially Sephardic and Mizrahi communities from Spain, Portugal, North Africa, and the Middle East— have incorporated this practice into a seder, traditionally conducted on the first night of Rosh Hashanah. It is called a *seder yehi ratzon* (may it be God's will), because we ask God to provide us with abundance, strength, and peace in the year ahead.

Food is a universal language. The Rosh Hashanah seder doesn't demand erudition or expertise. It is accessible to young and old, observant and secular. This version of the seder is the one my family conducted in our native Calcutta. We trace our ancestry to Baghdadi Jews from Iraq.

Seder means "order," so we eat the traditional foods in a prescribed order, offering a blessing specific to each food. The blessing may come from a characteristic of the food we would like to

emulate, such as the sweetness of the apple. Other blessings are based on word play, using words that sound like the Hebrew name of the food. Some blessings ask for the destruction of our enemies. I have left the original blessings intact in the Hebrew, but in the translations, I have added positive wishes for peace, friendship, and freedom. You might have to wait a few extra minutes before you eat dinner, but in that time you can literally "count your blessings."

Each of the sections includes a story, activity, and/or craft. You may wish to extend your seder with these additions or use them before or during the High Holiday period.

Rosh Hashanah, (Head of the Year), which is celebrated on the first and second days of the Hebrew month of Tishri, is both a serious and joyous time. We think about our actions in the past year, and prepare to greet the year ahead. It begins the Ten Days of Repentance that end on Yom Kippur, the Day of Atonement, when we request forgiveness from one another and ask God to inscribe us in the Book of Life. We wish one another Shanah Tovah, a good year!

In Sephardic and Mizrahi communities, a favorite greeting is, *tizkoo le-shanim rabot:*May you merit many years! The response *tizkeh ve-tihyeh ve'orekh* (for a male) or *tizkee vetihyee ve'orekh yamim* (for a female): May you merit life—long life!

Shopping List:

In addition to Wine and Hallah, you will need:

Pitted Dates
Pomegranate or Figs
Apples and Honey
Green Beans
Pumpkin or Gourd
Beetroot Leaves or Spinach
Leeks, Scallions, or Chives
Head of Lettuce

Preparing for the Seder

The foods at the seder can be prepared as simply or as elegantly as you wish. You may let the fruits or vegetables star as themselves, or mix them into delectable culinary creations. You will find many recipes at the back of the book.

Arrange eight bowls on a platter and fill them with the following fruits and vegetables:

1. Dates: Temarim

Split each date. Place a walnut in between to make a sandwich. Arrange them in a bowl or plate. Or bake date muffins.

2. Pomegranate: Rimon

Peel and remove all seeds from the pomegranate and place them in a bowl. It's fun to count them if you have the patience. Or toss them into a fruit salad. If you cannot find a pomegranate, substitute figs, which also have an abundance of seeds.

3. Apples in honey: Tapuah bi-d'vash

Here's where Ashkenazic and Sephardic tradition meet. Both serve sweetened apples for the new year. Some people use quinces which look like golden apples.

Slice apples and serve dipped in honey. Or create a traditional apple preserve by cooking apple quarters, until soft, in a small amount of water sweetened with sugar and spiced with whole cloves and rosewater. You can also serve the apples baked, stuffed with raisins and honey.

4. Green Beans: Rubia or Lubia

In India, where my family is from, we used lubia, a long bean pod with many seeds. It is similar to the rubia mentioned in the Talmud, and may even be the same vegetable. Lubia is available in Indian and Chinese grocery shops. Otherwise, substitute any kind of green bean. Boil beans and place in bowl. Serve topped with almonds if you like.

5. Pumpkin or Gourd: K'ra

Cook pumpkin or gourd until soft. Mash and sweeten to taste with brown sugar or honey, cinnamon, and ground cloves. Or just open a can of pumpkin pie filling. You can serve couscous with pumpkin and other vegetables, or even bake a pumpkin bread.

6. Beetroot Leaves or Spinach: Selek

Cut the leaves off the beets. Wash thoroughly and boil in a little water. If you choose spinach, make a spinach salad with sliced mushrooms, orange sections, dried cranberries, and alfalfa sprouts. Or make a spinach frittata.

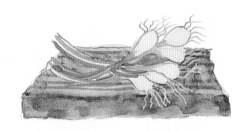

7. Leeks, Scallions, or Chives: Karti

Slice leeks or scallions or chop chives finely. If you use leeks, cook them in a little broth, or whip up some leek patties. In India, we used an herb called lusson grass, similar to chives.

8. Lettuce: Rosh ve-lo Zanav

Traditionally, the seder concludes with the head of a fish or a sheep. You may wish, instead, to consider the vegetarian alternative: a head of lettuce! Tear lettuce into bite-sized pieces. Use many varieties of lettuce and other greens and toss them into a salad.

A New Beginning

The verse that proclaims the New Year is from a *piyyut*, a religious poem, written by Abraham Hazzan Girondi. Each verse has a chorus that declares:

תִּכְלֶה שָׁנָה וְקִלְלוֹתֶיהָ!

Tikhleh shanah ve'killeloteha!

Let the year end with all its curses!

The last line reflects a change in tone:

תָּחֵל שָׁנָה וּבִרְכוֹתֶיהָ!

Tahel shanah u-virkhoteha!

Let the new year begin with all its blessings!

THINK! How are these wishes different?

How can we turn a curse into a blessing?

The Seder

Proclaim the beginning of the new year with the following verse:

תָּחֵל שָׁנָה וּבִרְכוֹתֶיהָ!

Tahel shanah u-virkhoteha!

Let the new year begin with all its blessings!

Kiddush: Blessing over the Day

Lift the cup of wine or grape juice and say:
(On Shabbat, add the words in parentheses:)

(וַיְהִי עֶרֶב וַיְהִי בֹקֶר יוֹם הַשִּׁשִּׁי. וַיְכֻלּוּ הַשָּׁמַיִם וְהָאָרֶץ וְכָל
צְבָאָם. וַיְכַל אֱלֹהִים בַּיּוֹם הַשְּׁבִיעִי מְלַאכְתּוֹ אֲשֶׁר עָשָׂה,
וַיִּשְׁבֹּת בַּיּוֹם הַשְּׁבִיעִי מִכָּל מְלַאכְתּוֹ אֲשֶׁר עָשָׂה. וַיְבָרֶךְ
אֱלֹהִים אֶת יוֹם הַשְּׁבִיעִי וַיְקַדֵּשׁ אֹתוֹ כִּי בוֹ שָׁבַת מִכָּל
מְלַאכְתּוֹ אֲשֶׁר בָּרָא אֱלֹהִים לַעֲשׂוֹת.)

(Va-yehi erev va-yehi voker yom ha-shishi.
Va-yekhulu ha-shamayim ve-ha-aretz ve-khol tzeva'am.
Va-yekhal Elohim ba-yom ha-sh'vi'i melakhto asher asah,
Va-yishbot ba-yom ha-sh'vi'i mi-kol melakhto asher asah.
Va-yevarekh Elohim et yom ha-sh'vi'i va-yekadesh oto
Ki vo shavat mi-kol melakhto asher bara Elohim la-asot.)

(On the sixth day, God completed the heavens and the earth.
On the seventh day, God finished creating the universe and rested.
God blessed the seventh day and made it holy.)

HAVDALAH (on Saturday night)

בָּרוּךְ אַתָּה יְיָ אֱלֹהֵינוּ מֶלֶךְ הָעוֹלָם, בּוֹרֵא מְאוֹרֵי הָאֵשׁ.

Barukh atah Adonai, eloheinu melekh ha-olam, borei me'orei ha-esh.

בָּרוּךְ אַתָּה יְיָ אֱלֹהֵינוּ מֶלֶךְ הָעוֹלָם, הַמַּבְדִּיל בֵּין קֹדֶשׁ לְקֹדֶשׁ.

Barukh atah Adonai, eloheinu melekh ha-olam, ha-mavdil bein kodesh le-kodesh.

Praised are You, Adonai our God, Who creates the lights of fire.
Praised are You, Adonai our God, Who separates the holiness of
Shabbat from the holiness of festivals.

Which Blessing?

One day Rabbi Joshua met a friend he hadn't seen in some time.
"My dear rabbi," the friend said. "I haven't seen you for more
than 30 days. What shall I say to you?"
"You should say a blessing," the rabbi answered.
"But which blessing would be appropriate?" the friend asked.
"The most appropriate would be the *Shehekheyanu:* Praised is
the One Who has kept us alive, sustained us, and brought us to
this occasion," the rabbi replied. (*Talmud, Berakhot* 58)

THINK! What does this story tell us about friendship?

What makes a good friend?

Can you be a friend to someone you haven't seen in a month?
A year?

[Note: this is the Sephardic version, which differs somewhat from the Ashkenazic text]

בָּרוּךְ אַתָּה יְיָ אֱלֹהֵינוּ מֶלֶךְ הָעוֹלָם, בּוֹרֵא פְּרִי הַגָּפֶן.
בָּרוּךְ אַתָּה יְיָ אֱלֹהֵינוּ מֶלֶךְ הָעוֹלָם, אֲשֶׁר בָּחַר בָּנוּ מִכָּל־עָם
וְרוֹמְמָנוּ מִכָּל־לָשׁוֹן וְקִדְּשָׁנוּ בְּמִצְוֹתָיו.   וַתִּתֶּן־לָנוּ יְיָ אֱלֹהֵינוּ
בְּאַהֲבָה (אֶת יוֹם הַמָּנוֹחַ הַזֶּה) אֶת יוֹם הַזִּכָּרוֹן הַזֶּה אֶת יוֹם
טוֹב מִקְרָא קֹדֶשׁ הַזֶּה (זִכְרוֹן תְּרוּעָה) יוֹם תְּרוּעָה בְּאַהֲבָה
מִקְרָא קֹדֶשׁ. זֵכֶר לִיצִיאַת מִצְרָיִם. וּדְבָרְךָ מַלְכֵּנוּ אֱמֶת וְקַיָּם
לָעַד.   בָּרוּךְ אַתָּה יְיָ מֶלֶךְ עַל כָּל־הָאָרֶץ מְקַדֵּשׁ (הַשַּׁבָּת
וְ)יִשְׂרָאֵל וְיוֹם הַזִּכָּרוֹן.

Barukh atah Adonai, eloheinu melekh ha-olam borei p'ri ha-gefen. Barukh atah Adonai, eloheinu melekh ha-olam, asher bahar banu mi-kol am ve-rom'manu mi-kol lashon ve-kid'shanu be-mitzvotav. Va-titen lanu Adonai eloheinu be-ahavah (et yom ha-manoah ha-zeh) et Yom Hazikaron ha-zeh, et yom tov mikra kodesh ha-zeh (zikhron teruah) yom teruah be-ahavah mikra kodesh. Zekher litziyat Mitzrayim. U-devarkha malkenu emet ve-kayam la'ad. Barukh atah Adonai melekh al kol ha-aretz, mekadesh (ha-Shabbat ve-) Yisrael ve-Yom Ha-Zikaron.

Praised are You, Adonai our God, Who creates the fruit of the vine. Praised are You, Adonai our God, Who has lifted us up through mitzvot and with love has given us (this Sabbath day of rest,) this Day of Remembrance, this festival day, a day of sounding the Shofar, recalling our leaving Egypt. Praised are You, Adonai our God, Who has set apart (Shabbat and) the people Israel and the Day of Remembrance.

If Rosh Hashanah begins on Saturday night, add Havdalah on page 12.

Shehekheyanu

בָּרוּךְ אַתָּה יְיָ אֱלֹהֵינוּ מֶלֶךְ הָעוֹלָם, שֶׁהֶחֱיָנוּ וְקִיְּמָנוּ
וְהִגִּיעָנוּ לַזְּמַן הַזֶּה.

*Barukh atah Adonai, eloheinu melekh ha-olam,
she-hekheyanu ve-ki'y'manu ve-higianu la-z'man ha-zeh.*

Praised are You, Adonai our God, Who has given us life and kept us well so we could celebrate this special time.

Drink the wine or grape juice.

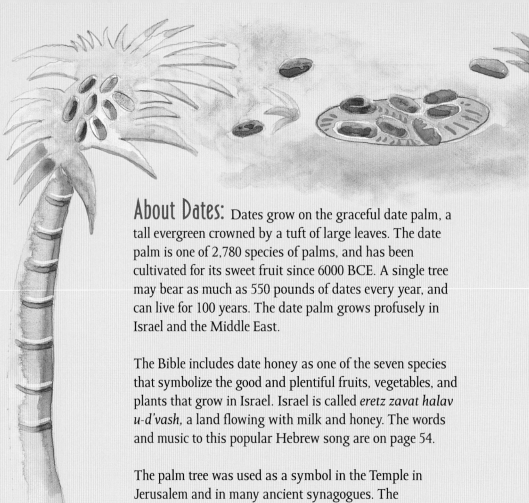

About Dates: Dates grow on the graceful date palm, a tall evergreen crowned by a tuft of large leaves. The date palm is one of 2,780 species of palms, and has been cultivated for its sweet fruit since 6000 BCE. A single tree may bear as much as 550 pounds of dates every year, and can live for 100 years. The date palm grows profusely in Israel and the Middle East.

The Bible includes date honey as one of the seven species that symbolize the good and plentiful fruits, vegetables, and plants that grow in Israel. Israel is called *eretz zavat halav u-d'vash*, a land flowing with milk and honey. The words and music to this popular Hebrew song are on page 54.

The palm tree was used as a symbol in the Temple in Jerusalem and in many ancient synagogues. The Maccabees used it as their insignia. On the holiday of Sukkot, we use a palm branch (*lulav*) as one of the four species, together with myrtle, willow, and citron (*etrog*). Several women in the Bible were named Tamar (Hebrew for date), and today it is still a popular girl's name.

THINK! Wishes are great, but how do we translate them into action?

What can you do to bring peace to your own family?

Your community?

Can one person help bring peace to the world?

Dates:
Temarim

A Wish For Peace

Pass around the bowl of dates and, before eating, recite together:

יְהִי רָצוֹן מִלְּפָנֶיךָ יְיָ אֱלֹהֵינוּ וֵאלֹהֵי אֲבוֹתֵינוּ (וְאִמּוֹתֵינוּ)
שֶׁיִּתַּמּוּ אוֹיְבֵינוּ וְשׂוֹנְאֵינוּ וְכָל מְבַקְשֵׁי רָעָתֵנוּ.

*Yehi ratzon mil'fanekha Adonai eloheinu v'elohei avoteinu (ve-imoteinu),
she-yitamu oyveinu ve-soneinu ve-khol mevakshei ra'ateinu.*

May it be Your will, God, that all enmity will end.

*As we eat this date, may we date this new year with happiness,
blessing, and peace for all.**

בָּרוּךְ אַתָּה יְיָ אֱלֹהֵינוּ מֶלֶךְ הָעוֹלָם, בּוֹרֵא פְּרִי הָעֵץ.

*Barukh atah Adonai, elohenu melekh
ha-olam, borei p'ri ha-etz.*

Blessed are You, Adonai, Ruler of
the universe, Who has created
the fruit of the tree.

Word Play

The word for "end,"
yitamu, sounds like
tamar, the Hebrew
word for date.

The Story of Deborah

Deborah sat under the palm tree and surveyed her people. It had been so many years since Moses died and Joshua had led the children of Israel into the land of Israel. Now she had become one of the judges whose job it was to guide the people to settle in the land and conquer it. She had come so far that people began to call her a prophetess!

Deborah had chosen the palm tree, a symbol of strength and grace, as the place people could come to her with questions and quarrels. It was where she held court, and judged what was right and wrong. People called the tree by her name, *Tomer Devorah,* Deborah's Date Tree. They said she was as strong, upright, and beautiful as the tree.

Deborah summoned her lieutenant Barak to discuss their struggles with Yavin, the king of Canaan, and his lieutenant, Sisera. "Go!" she told him. "Gather ten thousand men as God has commanded. We will fight back against Yavin's cruel rule." Barak and Deborah led the people into battle. They charged down Mt. Tabor, and God threw all of the enemy chariots into panic. The Canaanite soldiers fell by the sword—but Sisera escaped.

Sisera fled to the tent of Yael. Though she was the wife of Heber the Kenite, whose family was friendly to Yavin, Yael was loyal to the Israelites. She welcomed Sisera and gave him a glass of milk to make him drowsy. When he was asleep, Yael took a tent pin, pierced him through the temple, and killed him.

When word of Sisera's death came to Deborah under the palm tree, she rejoiced. She and Barak sang a song to God. "So may your enemies perish, God! Those who love God will be like the sun rising in all its glory."

About the Pomegranate:

The pomegranate is another of the seven species of Israel. In the Bible, literature, and art, it symbolizes beauty and fertility, because of its large scarlet flowers, glossy green leaves, round red fruit, and numerous seeds.

According to the rabbis, the pomegranate has 613 seeds, the number of *mitzvot* (commandments) in the Torah. The Talmud compares good study habits to the pomegranate: eat only the good fruit, but discard the bitter peel.

Bells shaped like pomegranates decorated the High Priest's robe in the Temple. King Solomon's crown was modeled after the crown of the pomegranate. The silver bells that are often placed on top of the wooden handles of the Torah are called *rimonim*, the Hebrew word for pomegranates. Many of these bells are shaped like the fruit. The modern state of Israel has used the pomegranate on its coins.

Many Hebrew songs tell of the fragrance and beauty of the pomegranate. You will find two of them on pages 55–56.

Pomegranate:
Rimon

A Wish For Mitzvot (Good Deeds)

Pass around the bowl of pomegranate seeds and, before eating, recite:

יְהִי רָצוֹן מִלְפָנֶיךָ יְיָ אֱלֹהֵינוּ וֵאלֹהֵי אֲבוֹתֵינוּ (וְאִמּוֹתֵינוּ)
שֶׁנִהְיֶה מְלֵאִים מִצְוֹת כָּרִמּוֹן.

Yehi ratzon mil'fanekha Adonai eloheinu v'elohei avoteinu (ve-imoteinu),
she-nihyeh m'le'im mitzvot ka-rimon.

May we be as full of good deeds
as the pomegranate is full of seeds.

THINK! Plants and people grow from tiny seeds, but they
also need nourishment.

How do you nourish a plant?

How would you nourish a person?

How would you nourish the world?

What is an extra mitzvah you'd like to do this coming year?

The Magic Pomegranate

Once there were three brothers who loved adventure. They decided
to go on a journey, each one to a different country. They agreed to
meet in ten years, and each would bring back an unusual gift.

The oldest brother went to the East. There, he saw magicians,
jugglers, and acrobats. One magician held up a magic glass through
which he could see the distant corners of the kingdom. The brother
bought the glass.

The middle brother traveled to the West. One day, he passed an old
carpet seller calling out his wares. When he looked at the pile of
colorful carpets, he saw one rug at the bottom begin to move. The
merchant whispered to him that this was a magic carpet that would
take him wherever he wanted to go. The brother bought the carpet.

The youngest brother went south, to a country noted for its many forests. In a grove of trees, he noticed a tree different from all the trees around it. It was covered with orange-red blossoms, and it was so beautiful! As he came closer, the brother noticed a single red pomegranate on the tree. When he reached for it, it fell into his hand, and another pomegranate burst into bloom in its place. The brother knew that this must be a magic pomegranate, but he wondered what kind of magic it performed. He put it into his pocket, and by the time he looked up again, the tree had disappeared.

When the brothers were reunited, they shared their gifts. The oldest brother held up his magic glass and saw, in a far-off kingdom, a young princess lying ill, near death.

"Hurry," said the middle brother. "Get on my magic carpet!" Seconds later, they arrived at the kingdom, and heard that the king had decreed that whoever cured his daughter could have her hand in marriage.

The youngest brother asked if he could try. He cut open his pomegranate and fed the juicy kernels to the princess. Soon, she felt stronger and her cheeks bloomed. The king was overjoyed. But the brothers began to argue over who had saved the princess.

"If it weren't for my magic glass, we never would have known the princess was ill," said the oldest.

"If it weren't for my magic carpet, we wouldn't have arrived in time to save her," said the middle brother.

"But my magic pomegranate actually healed her," said the youngest.

The king asked the princess who she thought was most deserving. She asked the oldest brother, "Has your magic glass changed in any way since you arrived in the kingdom?"

"No," he answered.

She turned to the middle brother. "Has your magic carpet changed in any way since you arrived?" she asked.

"No," he answered.

"Has your magic pomegranate changed?" she asked the third brother.

"Yes," he answered. "It's no longer whole, since I gave you half of it."

"I will marry the youngest brother," said the princess, "because he performed the greatest good deed—he gave up something of his own."

A lavish wedding followed, and the princess and all three brothers became the king's royal advisers.

About the Apple:
The apple is often called the "king of fruits." Its trees flourish in more parts of the earth than any other fruit tree. Charred remains of apples have been found in ruins of prehistoric dwellings. There are even Stone Age carvings of them! Apples originated in Asia, and were probably brought to England by the Romans. The colonists brought them to America, which is today the world's leader in apple production. There are thousands of varieties of apples, glossy and crisp, and so good to eat!

Did you know that the fruit Eve ate in the Bible was probably not an apple? It is not given a name in the biblical story. The rabbis suggested that the fruit may have been grapes, a fig, a citron *(etrog)*, or possibly wheat.

Some scholars say that biblical references to *tapuah* (usually translated as apple) actually refer to the quince, which looks like a golden apple and grows widely in the Middle East.

The sages compare Israel to an apple tree: The apple tree blossoms before its leaves appear. So Israel agreed to do good deeds before it was commanded to.

Apples in Honey:
Tapuah Bi-d'vash

A Wish for Sweetness

Pass around the apple and before eating, recite:

יְהִי רָצוֹן מִלְפָנֶיךָ יְיָ אֱלֹהֵינוּ וֵאלֹהֵי אֲבוֹתֵינוּ (וְאִמוֹתֵינוּ)
שֶׁתְּחַדֵּשׁ עָלֵינוּ שָׁנָה טוֹבָה וּמְתוּקָה כַּדְּבַשׁ מֵרֵאשִׁית
הַשָּׁנָה וְעַד אַחֲרִית הַשָּׁנָה.

*Yehi ratzon mil'fanekha Adonai eloheinu v'elohei avoteinu (ve-imoteinu),
she-tehadesh aleinu shanah tovah u-metukah ka-d'vash, me-reishit ha-shanah
ve-ad aharit ha-shanah.*

May it be Your will, God, to renew for us a year as good and sweet
as honey, from the beginning of the year all the way to its end.

THINK! Beginnings are often difficult. That's why we try
to make them as smooth and sweet as possible. In many Jewish
communities, it was a custom to write the Hebrew alphabet in
honey on a child's slate when he or she began school, to
symbolize the hope that the words of Torah be sweet. Today, we
often give children cookies when they start Hebrew school.

Can you think of a beginning, a "first," that was hard for you?
What did you do to make it easier?

The Apple Tree's Discovery

In a great oak forest where the trees grew tall and majestic, a little apple tree stood alone.

Winter came. As the snow fell to the forest floor, it covered the branches of the apple tree. One night the apple tree looked up into the sky and saw a wonderful sight. The stars in the sky seemed to be hanging from the branches of the oak trees.

"Oh, God," whispered the apple tree, "how lucky those oak trees are to have such beautiful stars hanging on their branches. I want more than anything to have stars on my branches. Then I would feel truly special."

God looked down and said gently, "Have patience! Have patience, little apple tree."

Time passed. The snows melted and spring came to the land. Tiny white and pink blossoms appeared on the branches of the little apple tree. All summer long, the apple tree continued to grow, but night after night, when it looked up at the sky and saw the millions of stars, it cried again, "Oh, God, I wish I had stars on my branches and in my leaves."

God said, "You already have many gifts. Isn't it enough to offer shade to people, and fragrant blossoms and branches for birds to nest on?"

The apple tree sighed. "I don't mean to sound ungrateful, but stars would make me feel truly special."

Summer came and the apple tree filled with fruit. Again it asked God for stars, and God said, "Isn't it enough that you have such wonderful apples to offer?"

The apple tree shook its branches from side to side. At that moment God caused a wind to blow. The tree began to sway, and an apple fell from the top of the tree. When it hit the ground, it split open.

"Look," commanded God, "look inside yourself. What do you see?"

The little apple tree looked down and saw that right in the middle of the apple—was a star! "A star! I have a star!" the tree shouted excitedly.

God laughed a gentle laugh. "You do have stars, and they've been there all along. You just didn't know it!"

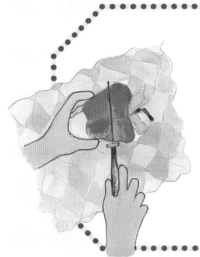

Activity:

Find the apple's star. Instead of cutting the apple with its stem up, turn it on its side and cut it across.

We can find the star inside of each of us if we change direction—just a little bit.

At this point in the seder, the sweet foods have been replaced with vegetables. If some of these are unfamiliar to you, it's good to know that the smallest bite is enough to fulfill the requirements of reciting the blessing.

About Green Beans:
More than 500 varieties of beans are cultivated throughout the world. Some are eaten with the pods, some are shelled and eaten, and some are harvested and dried. There are yellow beans and flat lima beans, navy beans used in baked beans, fat fava beans, and black-eyed peas that grow in a slender pod. Chinese long beans can measure one to three feet. Green beans are the most popular garden bean. They are low in calories, and high in vitamin A, C, and folate.

THINK! In Ashkenazic communities, it's a Rosh Hashanah tradition to eat carrots cut into round, golden "coins" as a symbol of prosperity. The Yiddish word for carrot, *mer*, is also the word for "more." Though we wish for "plenty" for ourselves, we also remember those who have less. What can we do to help make their lives better?

Two organizations that help people in need:

Mazon: A Jewish Response to Hunger (310) 442-0020 www.mazon.org

Ziv Tzedakah Fund (973) 763-9396 www.ziv.org

Green Beans: Rubia or Lubia

A Wish for Prosperity

Pass around beans and before eating, recite:

יְהִי רָצוֹן מִלְּפָנֶיךָ יְיָ אֱלֹהֵינוּ וֵאלֹהֵי אֲבוֹתֵינוּ (וְאִמוֹתֵינוּ)
שֶׁיִּרְבּוּ זְכֻיוֹתֵינוּ.

*Yehi ratzon mil'fanekha Adonai eloheinu
v'elohei avoteinu (ve-imoteinu), she-yirbu zekhuyoteinu.*

May it be Your will, God, that our merits increase.

בָּרוּךְ אַתָּה יְיָ אֱלֹהֵינוּ מֶלֶךְ הָעוֹלָם, בּוֹרֵא פְּרִי הָאֲדָמָה.

*Barukh atah Adonai eloheinu melekh ha-olam
borei p'ri ha-adamah.*

Blessed are You, Adonai, Ruler of the universe, Who has created the fruit of the earth.

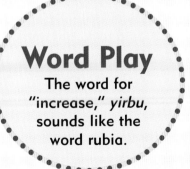

Word Play
The word for "increase," *yirbu*, sounds like the word rubia.

Jacob and the Beanstalk

Jacob lived in the land of Canaan with his mother and their dairy cow. They were so poor that they often had little more than milk to drink.

One day, Jacob's mother threw her hands up in despair. "There is nothing to eat!" she declared. "Go, Jacob, and sell the cow in the market!"

Jacob loved the cow, but he didn't argue. He took the cow and walked towards the village. On the way, he met an old man.

"I will give you three magic beans for that lovely cow," the man offered. Jacob wondered how the man knew he was on his way to sell the cow.

"Three magic beans!" Jacob thought to himself. "That will surely be better than the few coins I will get in the market!"

Jacob made the trade, but when he arrived home, his mother was not pleased. "Three beans?" she yelled, tossing them out the window. "What kind of dinner will we get from three beans?"

That night, Jacob couldn't sleep. He tossed and turned. His pillow felt as hard as a rock. He went outside, lay down on the ground and looked at the stars in the sky. "Maybe if I count them I will get sleepy," he said. "One, two, three . . . " When Jacob got to 101, he fell asleep.

In his sleep, he dreamed. He dreamed that the magic beans grew into three stalks. Two stalks grew side by side, tall and straight, and the third twined around the other two. The three beanstalks looked like a ladder reaching to the tops of the clouds.

Jacob fell into a deeper sleep. He even began snoring. Then he dreamed that angels were climbing up and down the beanstalk ladder. A voice from the tops of the clouds, quiet as a whisper, but booming like thunder at the same time, called out, "Don't worry, Jacob. I will protect you. You will prosper and provide for your family."

Jacob woke up suddenly. He opened one eye, then another, trembling at the memory of the dream. In front of him were three huge beanstalks laden not only with beans, but with tomatoes, cucumbers, squash, and every kind of vegetable imaginable. "I will call this the Garden of God," said Jacob. He tended the garden lovingly all his life, and his family never lacked for food again.

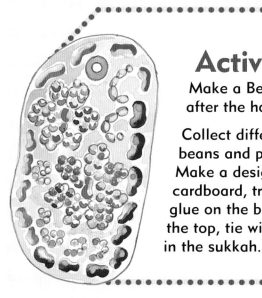

Activity:

Make a Bean Mosaic (before or after the holiday):

Collect different kinds of dried beans and peas.
Make a design on white cardboard, trace it with glue, and glue on the beans. Punch a hole at the top, tie with string, and hang it in the sukkah.

About the Gourd or Pumpkin:
The large, orange pumpkin is actually a fruit. Its plant has rough, heart-shaped leaves with yellow flowers. Pumpkins can grow up to giant sizes of one hundred pounds or more. The pumpkin is related to the squash and gourd families. Gourds are hard-shelled fruit that grow in many shapes, sizes, and colors and are used for decoration.

Counting Blessings
Rabbi Mani was troubled by his wealthy in-laws. "My wife's family really bothers me," he complained to his teacher, Rabbi Isaac ben Eliashav.

"I will say a prayer that they will become poor," Rabbi Isaac said. Amazingly, that's exactly what happened.

Sometime later, Rabbi Mani complained again. Now his wife's relatives were constantly asking for money.

"I will say a prayer that they will become rich again," his teacher agreed. Amazingly, their riches were restored.

Then Rabbi Mani complained about his wife Hannah. "She is ugly," he said. So Rabbi Isaac prayed for her to become beautiful, and she did. But even that didn't satisfy Rabbi Mani, because now his wife had become bossy.

"This is my last prayer," Rabbi Isaac said. "I will pray for Hannah to become ugly again." When Rabbi Mani returned home, his wife was as she used to be. He realized how foolish he had been, and finally, he was content. (*Talmud, Ta'anit 23b*)

THINK! Do you like to complain? It's often much easier to complain than to realize we can actually be happy. Rosh Hashanah is a chance to count our blessings and our merits.

Name three good things about you and your family.

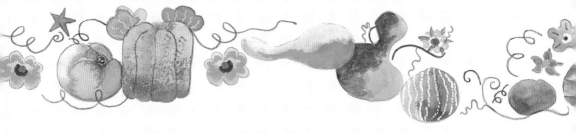

Pumpkin or Gourd: K'ra

A Wish for Happiness

Pass around pumpkin and before eating, recite:

יְהִי רָצוֹן מִלְפָנֶיךָ יְיָ אֱלֹהֵינוּ וֵאלֹהֵי אֲבוֹתֵינוּ (וְאִמּוֹתֵינוּ)
שֶׁתִּקְרַע רֹעַ גְזַר דִּנֵנוּ וְיִקָרְאוּ לְפָנֶיךָ זְכֻיּוֹתֵינוּ.

*Yehi ratzon mil'fanekha Adonai eloheinu v'elohei avoteinu (ve-imoteinu),
she-tikra ro'a g'zar dineinu ve-yikar'u lefanekha
zekhuyoteinu.*

May it be Your will, God, to tear away all evil decrees against us as our merits are proclaimed in front of You.

Guard us, God, as we eat of this gourd, if enemies gird at us in the year to come.*

Word Play

K'ra, the word for pumpkin, sounds like the word *kara*, which when spelled with the letter *ayin* means "tear away," and when spelled with the letter *alef* means "proclaimed."

The Story of Jonah

Once upon a time there was a city named Nineveh so full of wickedness that God decided to destroy the city unless the people changed their ways.

God chose a man named Jonah to be the messenger, but Jonah didn't believe the people of Nineveh were worthy, so he tried to escape by boarding a boat to Tarshish instead. God created a powerful storm that rocked the ship violently. Jonah wailed to his fellow travelers. "It's my fault. Throw me overboard!" The sailors did so, and as soon as Jonah's body touched the water, the storm subsided and the waters grew calm.

Just then, a fish, huge as a whale, spotted Jonah and gulped him down. In the smelly darkness of the fish's belly, Jonah prayed to God. "Save me!" he cried. "I promise to obey You." God commanded the fish to spit Jonah out onto dry land.

Jonah went to Nineveh and told the people: "Stop doing evil deeds! If you don't, your city will be destroyed in forty days!"

The king of Nineveh believed Jonah and told his people to fast and pray for forgiveness. God saw the people had repented and decided not to destroy the city. But Jonah got angry. "That's why I ran away the first time!" he said. "I knew You were too forgiving. I'm so embarrassed now I'd rather die!"

Jonah left and camped out behind the city. God caused a gourd to grow over Jonah's head to protect him from the hot sun. Jonah was comforted. But the next day, God caused a worm to attack the gourd and it withered. The sun beat down heavily on Jonah's head and he was faint. "It's better for me to die than live!" he cried.

"Why are you so upset about this plant which you did not tend or grow?" God asked. "It appeared overnight and died overnight. Shouldn't I, then, care about the great city of Nineveh, full of people whom I created?"

Because the story of Jonah deals with forgiveness, we read it on Yom Kippur afternoon.

Activity:

Hollow out a pumpkin and put a plant inside to make a centerpiece for your Rosh Hashanah table.

About Beets:

Both parts of the beet are edible—the red bulbous roots and the red-veined, dark-green leaves. In fact, the beet was originally grown for its leaves. According to early historians, the Romans ate only the tops, reserving the roots for medicinal purposes. The green leaves are nutritious, packed with vitamins A and C. Steam and serve them as you would spinach. The roots have a high natural sugar content but are low in calories, and rich in iron and vitamins. They may be steamed or baked, eaten hot or cold.

Turning Curses Into Blessings

When Balak, King of Moav, saw the strong band of Israelites approach, he feared for his people. So he sent for Bil'am, the most powerful wizard of the time. "Curse the Israelites," he ordered him, "and your reward will be great." But God put words in Bil'am's mouth and when he began to speak, a blessing spilled from his lips: "How goodly are your tents, O Jacob! Your dwellings, O Israel!" (Bemidbar 22:2–24:25)

THINK! Many of the blessings express wishes for harsh things to happen to those who try to harm us.

What situations might lead you to wish bad things for others?

Whom do you count as your enemies?

Without enemies, do we automatically have freedom?

What are some of the freedoms you enjoy?

How can we turn curses into blessings?

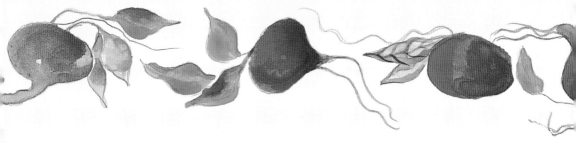

Beetroot Leaves:
Selek

A Wish for Freedom

Pass around spinach or beetroot leaves, and before eating, recite:

יְהִי רָצוֹן מִלְּפָנֶיךָ יְיָ אֱלֹהֵינוּ וֵאלֹהֵי אֲבוֹתֵינוּ (וְאִמּוֹתֵינוּ)
שֶׁיִּסְתַּלְּקוּ אוֹיְבֵינוּ וְשׂוֹנְאֵינוּ וְכָל מְבַקְשֵׁי רָעָתֵנוּ.

*Yehi ratzon mil'fanekha Adonai eloheinu v'elohei avoteinu (ve-imoteinu)
she-yistalku oyveinu ve-son'einu ve-khol m'vakshei ra'ateinu.*

May it be Your will, God, that all the enemies
who might beat us will beat a retreat, and
we will beat a path to freedom.

*As we bite this beet, may those who in
the past have beaten us or sought us
harm, beat to cover in the coming year.**

Word Play

Selek, the word for
beet, sounds like the
word *"yistalku,"* which
means "to beat a
retreat."

Tuli's Treasure

Two brothers, one rich, one poor, lived in the same town. The rich brother, who lived in a house with fourteen rooms, ate a seven-course meal each night for dinner. Did he share what he had with his brother? Not a chance.

The poor brother lived in a two-room cottage. He barely managed to feed his family with what he earned, but he always made sure he had enough left over to feed the animals. Every morning, he filled a bowl of milk for two stray cats who rubbed against his legs in appreciation. One day, they meowed so loudly that he decided to follow them. As he went deeper into the woods, more and more cats joined them until there was a procession of seven cats. They led him to a cave.

In the middle of the cave sat the biggest cat he ever saw. He was snowy white with black paws and a black mask around his green eyes.

"Welcome," said the cat. "I am Tuli, the King of the Cats. I have heard how kind you have been to my brothers. These are for you." King Tuli pointed to three sacks. The poor man was overjoyed when he saw that the bags were overflowing with food. One was filled with beets; the second, with garlic; the third, with carrots.

"We'll have a good dinner tonight!" he thought, and thanked King Tuli and all the cats. But when he arrived home and opened the bags, he gasped. Instead of beets, out spilled brilliant sapphires; instead of garlic, garnets; instead of carrots, ten-carat diamonds.

On the eve of Rosh Hashanah, the poor brother invited the rich brother and his family to his house for dinner. "What could they possibly feed us?" mused the rich brother scornfully. "We will probably come home starving!" He agreed to attend, but ordered his cook to have a second dinner ready when they returned.

When the rich man arrived at his brother's house, he found the table laden with fruits and vegetables, soups and meats of all kinds, cakes and cookies and pastries. He listened in amazement to the poor brother's story of his good fortune.

"No time for dinner. I must find that cave!" he exclaimed, and rushed off.

He stumbled upon the two stray cats and gave them a kick. "Lead me to the cave," he demanded. The cats complied.

When he reached the cave, the rich brother bellowed at King Tuli. "Give me the same bags you gave my brother!" Tuli simply pointed at three bags. The brother peered inside. Satisfied that they, too, were filled with beets, garlic, and carrots, he left. Tuli smiled to himself.

As soon as he was outside the cave, the rich brother tore open the bags, expecting to find diamonds and sapphires. But instead of carrots, out fell crabs; instead of beets, vicious bees; instead of garlic, garish, green-eyed snakes. The man ran as fast as he could, but he couldn't escape the stings and bites. When he finally got home, he wasn't even hungry for dinner.

Activity:

With the help of an adult, slice a roasted beet, and cut it into a heart or any other shape. Be careful handling it, because the beet will turn everything pink! Use it as a stamp for place cards or New Year's cards.

About Onions, Leeks, Scallions, and Chives: The onion, which is native to southwestern Asia, may get its name from the Latin word *unus*, meaning one. The ancient Egyptians thought the round bulb of the onion symbolized the universe. A member of the lily family, the onion has four hundred varieties. It grows as a bulb in the ground and is used in cooking and as a cure for many illnesses. Scallions, or green onions, are pulled before they mature. Leeks, a vegetable related to the onion, have a milder, sweeter flavor and supply potassium and vitamins A, C, and E. In the garden, leeks repel insects, so are often planted near carrots. Chives are the smallest and subtlest-flavored of the onion family. Chop its fresh, slender leaves into garnishes for salads, soups, sauces, omelets, stews, and mild cheeses.

When you cut an onion, it releases an irritating chemical that makes you cry. Here are some popular remedies—with no promise of effectiveness!

- *Put the onion in the refrigerator for 30 minutes before chopping.*
- *Put it in the freezer for 5-10 minutes.*
- *Heat it.*
- *Cut it under or near running water.*
- *Chop near a fan or other circulating air.*
- *Wear goggles.*
- *Put a piece of bread, raw potato, lemon wedge or sugar cube in your mouth while you cut.*
- *Light a candle nearby.*
- *Use a very sharp knife.*
- *Use a food processor.*
- *Choose sweet varieties that are not as pungent.*

Leeks, Scallions, or Chives: Karti

A Wish for Friendship

Pass around leeks, scallions, or chives and before eating, recite:

יְהִי רָצוֹן מִלְּפָנֶיךָ יְיָ אֱלֹהֵינוּ וֵאלֹהֵי אֲבוֹתֵינוּ (וְאִמוֹתֵינוּ)
שֶׁיִּכָּרְתוּ אוֹיְבֵינוּ וְשׂוֹנְאֵינוּ וְכָל מְבַקְשֵׁי רָעָתֵנוּ.

*Yehi ratzon mil'fanekha Adonai eloheinu v'elohei avoteinu (ve-imoteinu)
she-yikartu oyveinu ve-son'einu ve-khol mevakshei ra'ateinu.*

May it be Your will, God, that our enemies
be cut off. Without enemies, we hope for
the blessing of friendship.

*Like we eat this leek may our luck never
lack in the year to come.**

Word Play
Karti, the word for
leek, sounds like
"*yikartu*," the word
for "cut off."

THINK! What other foods can you think of that symbolize
wishes we have for the new year? For example, the olive branch
is a symbol of peace. So if you ate olives, you could say "May
we all live together peacefully."

Can you think of other wishes symbolized by your favorite fruits
and vegetables?

Two at a Time

Once upon a time, a cruel ruler played a wicked joke on the Jews who lived in his land. He decreed that they had to solve three riddles, or else they would be put to death.

Riders galloped throughout the land, proclaiming, "The king has decreed: These three things you must do, all at the same time. Appear before me clothed and naked; riding and walking; laughing and crying."

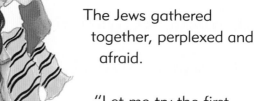

The Jews gathered together, perplexed and afraid.

"Let me try the first riddle," said Esther. "I know about fashion." She put on every piece of clothing in her closet, but she couldn't solve the riddle.

44

"Let me try the second riddle," said Sarah, who owned a stable. She stood on top of her favorite horse and tried walking a few steps, but the horse shook herself, and Sarah fell off.

"Let me try the third riddle," said Natan, who had been married four times. He looked at each of his ex-wives, but all he could do was cry.

Nobody knew how to solve the riddles. They called a fast day. Nothing was eaten from one evening until the next.

Suddenly a little girl came forward. "Don't worry," she said. "I have the solution." But she refused to tell anyone what she was going to do, not even her own mother.

When the day came, she rode before the king on the back of her baby donkey, who was so small that the little girl's feet touched the floor, so she walked as she rode. She wore a net, so that she was both clothed and naked. And with her hands she peeled an onion so that her eyes overflowed with tears. Yet she was laughing, because she knew she had saved her people.

Why Lettuce?

Traditionally, the seder concludes with the head of a fish or a sheep. If a sheep is used, the brains are removed and cooked into a savory dish called sweetbreads. The sheep's head is a tangible symbol of our wish to be heads, not tails, leaders, not stragglers. It also serves as a reminder of the binding of Isaac, the biblical story we read on Rosh Hashanah. It was a ram that was sacrificed in place of Isaac. A fish is seen as a symbol of God's protection; a fish's eyes never close, as God is always watchful. Some communities, however, discontinued using the fish head because of the similarity between the Hebrew words for fish (*dag*) and worry (*d'agah*). Today, many choose to use a head of lettuce.

The Proper Place for a Tail

A snake went slithering down the road.

"How long will you insist on leading while I drag along behind you!" cried the tail to the head. "Why shouldn't we change places for once? Let me lead now and you follow."

"Very well," agreed the head. "You go first." So the tail began to lead and the head trailed after.

At last they came to a pit filled with water and the tail, not having any eyes, slid right into the pit, dragging the head along with it. It fell among sharp thorns and hurt itself as well as the head.

Now, I ask, who was to blame? Didn't it serve the head right for being so weak that it allowed itself to be led by a brainless tail?

Head of
Lettuce

A Wish For Leadership

Pass around the lettuce and before eating, recite:

יְהִי רָצוֹן מִלְּפָנֶיךָ יְיָ אֱלֹהֵינוּ וֵאלֹהֵי אֲבוֹתֵינוּ (וְאִמוֹתֵינוּ)
שֶׁנִּהְיֶה לְראשׁ וְלֹא לְזָנָב.

*Yehi ratzon mil'fanekha Adonai eloheinu v'elohei avoteinu (ve-imoteinu)
she-nih'yeh le-rosh ve-lo le-zanav.*

May it be Your will, God,
that we will be heads and not tails, leaders instead of followers.

THINK! Is it harder to be a leader or a follower? Why?

Rosh means "head" in Hebrew. Our heads are home to our eyes, ears, nose, and mouth. How do seeing, hearing, smelling, and speaking help us to be good leaders?

Breaking Bread:

The *motzi*, the blessing over bread, reminds us not to take our food for granted. We thank God for the most basic of food—bread—which originates in grain that springs from the earth.

Once the Temple in ancient Jerusalem was destroyed, the tables in our own homes came to symbolize the altar, the holiest place in the Temple. Just as the sacrifices in the Temple were sprinkled with salt, so we, too, usually sprinkle salt over the hallah on Shabbat and holidays. At Rosh Hashanah, it's a custom to substitute sugar or honey.

Some people have a custom of eating a new fruit on Rosh Hashanah, one that they have not tasted in over a month. They recite the *shehekheyanu* blessing (see page 13). From the most earthly to the most exotic, all food is a blessing.

THE MEAL

Netilat Yadayim: Washing Hands

Pass around a pitcher of water, a bowl, and a towel. Hold the pitcher in one hand and pour water over the other. Reverse hands and repeat. Dry your hands and recite:

בָּרוּךְ אַתָּה יְיָ אֱלֹהֵינוּ מֶלֶךְ הָעוֹלָם, אֲשֶׁר קִדְּשָׁנוּ בְּמִצְוֹתָיו וְצִוָּנוּ עַל נְטִילַת יָדָיִם.

Barukh atah Adonai, eloheinu melekh ha-olam, asher kid'shanu be-mitzvotav ve-tzivanu al netilat yadayim.

Praised are You, Adonai our God, Who has commanded us to cleanse our hands and lift up our spirits before we eat.

Motzi: Blessing over the Bread

בָּרוּךְ אַתָּה יְיָ אֱלֹהֵינוּ מֶלֶךְ הָעוֹלָם, הַמּוֹצִיא לֶחֶם מִן הָאָרֶץ.

Barukh atah Adonai, eloheinu melekh ha-olam, ha-motzi lehem min ha-aretz.

Praised are You, Adonai our God, Who brings forth bread from the earth.

תָּחֵל שָׁנָה וּבִרְכוֹתֶיהָ!

Tahel shanah u-virkhoteha!

May the year ahead be full of blessings!

Enjoy your meal!

Birkat Ha-mazon
(Blessing after Meals—abbreviated)

Like the shape of the world, our meal is a circle. We began with the *motzi* blessing, giving thanks for our food, and we end with *Birkat Ha-mazon*, blessings after the meal. We thank God for providing food for all living things and for all that is good. We ask God for life and health. We thank God for the land of Israel and pray for a rebuilt Jerusalem. We ask God to renew us for another good year and to bless us with peace.

בָּרוּךְ אַתָּה יְיָ אֱלֹהֵינוּ מֶלֶךְ הָעוֹלָם, הַזָּן אֶת הָעוֹלָם כֻּלּוֹ בְּטוּבוֹ,
בְּחֵן בְּחֶסֶד וּבְרַחֲמִים. הוּא נוֹתֵן לֶחֶם לְכָל בָּשָׂר, כִּי לְעוֹלָם
חַסְדּוֹ. וּבְטוּבוֹ הַגָּדוֹל תָּמִיד לֹא חָסַר לָנוּ, וְאַל יֶחְסַר לָנוּ מָזוֹן
לְעוֹלָם וָעֶד בַּעֲבוּר שְׁמוֹ הַגָּדוֹל כִּי הוּא אֵל זָן וּמְפַרְנֵס לַכֹּל,
וּמֵטִיב לַכֹּל, וּמֵכִין מָזוֹן לְכָל בְּרִיּוֹתָיו אֲשֶׁר בָּרָא. בָּרוּךְ אַתָּה יְיָ
הַזָּן אֶת הַכֹּל.

Barukh atah Adonai, eloheinu melekh ha-olam, ha-zan et ha-olam kulo be-tuvo, be-hen, be-hesed, u-v'rahamim. Hu notein lehem le-khol basar, ki le-olam hasdo. U-v'tuvo ha-gadol, tamid lo hasar lanu, ve-al yehsar lanu mazon le-olam va-ed, ba-avur shemo ha-gadol, ki hu el zan u-m'farnes la-kol, u-meitiv la-kol, u-meikhin mazon le-khol b'riyotav asher bara. Barukh atah Adonai, ha-zan et ha-kol.

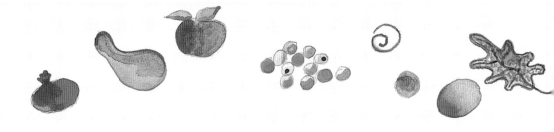

נוֹדֶה לְּךָ יְיָ אֱלֹהֵינוּ עַל שֶׁהִנְחַלְתָּ לַאֲבוֹתֵינוּ אֶרֶץ חֶמְדָּה טוֹבָה
וּרְחָבָה, בְּרִית וְתוֹרָה, חַיִּים וּמָזוֹן. יִתְבָּרַךְ שִׁמְךָ בְּפִי כָּל חַי
תָּמִיד לְעוֹלָם וָעֶד, כַּכָּתוּב: וְאָכַלְתָּ וְשָׂבָעְתָּ, וּבֵרַכְתָּ אֶת יְיָ
אֱלֹהֶיךָ עַל הָאָרֶץ הַטּוֹבָה אֲשֶׁר נָתַן לָךְ. בָּרוּךְ אַתָּה יְיָ, עַל
הָאָרֶץ וְעַל הַמָּזוֹן.

Nodeh l'kha Adonai eloheinu al she-hinhalta l'avoteinu eretz hemdah tovah u-r'hava,
b'rit ve-Torah, hayyim u-mazon. Yitbarakh shimkha be-fi kol hai tamid le-olam va-ed.
Ka-katuv ve-akhalta, ve-savata, u-verakhta et Adonai elohekha, al ha-aretz ha-tovah
asher natan lakh. Barukh atah Adonai, al ha-aretz ve-al ha-mazon.

וּבְנֵה יְרוּשָׁלַיִם עִיר הַקֹּדֶשׁ בִּמְהֵרָה בְיָמֵינוּ. בָּרוּךְ אַתָּה יְיָ, בּוֹנֵה
בְרַחֲמָיו יְרוּשָׁלַיִם, אָמֵן.

U-v'nei Yerushalayim ir ha-kodesh bi-m'herah ve-yameinu. Barukh atah Adonai, bonei
ve-rahamav Yerushalayim. Amen.

בָּרוּךְ אַתָּה יְיָ אֱלֹהֵינוּ מֶלֶךְ הָעוֹלָם, הַמֶּלֶךְ הַטּוֹב וְהַמֵּטִיב לַכֹּל,
הוּא הֵטִיב, הוּא מֵטִיב, הוּא יֵיטִיב לָנוּ. הוּא גְמָלָנוּ, הוּא
גוֹמְלֵנוּ, הוּא יִגְמְלֵנוּ לָעַד, חֵן וָחֶסֶד וְרַחֲמִים, וִיזַכֵּנוּ לִימוֹת
הַמָּשִׁיחַ.

Barukh atah Adonai, eloheinu melekh ha-olam, ha-melekh ha-tov ve-ha-meitiv lakol.
Hu heitiv, hu meitiv, hu yeitiv lanu. Hu g'malanu, hu gom'leinu, hu yig'm'leinu la'ad,
hen va-hesed ve-rahamim, vi-zakeinu limot ha-mashiah.

הָרַחֲמָן, הוּא יְחַדֵּשׁ עָלֵינוּ אֶת הַשָּׁנָה הַזֹּאות לְטוֹבָה וְלִבְרָכָה.

Ha-rahaman hu yehadesh aleinu et ha-shanah ha-zot le-tovah ve-liv'rakhah.

עֹשֶׂה שָׁלוֹם בִּמְרוֹמָיו, הוּא יַעֲשֶׂה שָׁלוֹם עָלֵינוּ וְעַל כָּל יִשְׂרָאֵל,
וְאִמְרוּ אָמֵן.

Oseh shalom bi-m'romav, hu ya'aseh shalom aleinu ve-al kol Yisrael, ve-imru amen.

New Year's Food Customs Around the World

Food is a universal language. Communities around the world, of all traditions and religions, eat special, symbolic foods at their New Year's celebrations.

The Japanese eat buckwheat noodles that symbolize long life. Children try to swallow at least one noodle whole for good luck.

Black-eyed peas and collard greens are popular New Year's fare in the American South because they symbolize prosperity: the peas look like little coins and swell as they cook; the greens are the color of money.

For a lucky, fruitful year, Latin Americans and those of Spanish descent eat twelve grapes at midnight on New Year's Eve.

In Greece, it's a tradition to eat *vasilopita*, a cake baked with a coin inside. The person who bites into his piece of cake and finds the coin is said to be blessed with good luck. (Not recommended!)

At the Persian New Year, a table is set with seven items, all starting with the Farsi letter "seen": green vegetables, garlic, vinegar, dried fruit, a hyacinth flower, coins, and a snack made from flour and sugar.

The Chinese enjoy cookies, oranges, and orange-inspired dishes that symbolize sweetness and good fortune, as well as "pot stickers," dumplings that look like ancient Chinese coins. The Chinese also have a feast that features dishes whose names or ingredients sound like wishes for the new year. The word for turnips also means "good luck" in some dialects; the word for fish sounds like the word for plenty.

Sound familiar?

Eretz Zavat Halav U-d'vash

אֶרֶץ זָבַת חָלָב וּדְבָשׁ

A land flowing
with milk and honey.

El Ginat Egoz

Music: S. Levi Tanai
Lyrics: Song of Songs

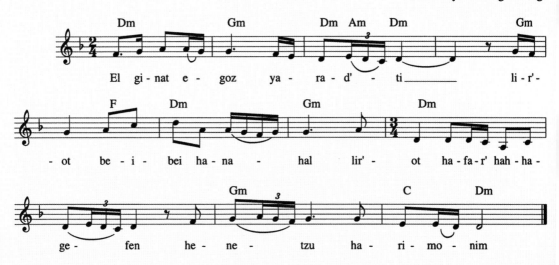

El gi - nat e - goz ya - ra - d' - ti___ li - r'- - ot be - i - bei ha - na - hal lir' - ot ha - fa - r' hah - ha - ge - fen he - ne - tzu ha - ri - mo - nim

אֶל־גִּנַּת אֱגוֹז יָרַדְתִּי
לִרְאוֹת בְּאִבֵּי הַנָּחַל
לִרְאוֹת הֲפָרְחָה הַגֶּפֶן
הֵנֵצוּ הָרִמֹּנִים.

I went down to the garden to look
at the plants, to see whether the grapes
and the pomegranates had flowered.

55

Etz Ha-rimon

Persian melody

Etz ha-ri-mon na-tan rei-ho bein yam ha-me-lah ad Ye-ri-ho shav ho-ma-ti___ g'du-dekh___ min-dod shav ta-ma-ti do-dekh mi-dod otz-rot O-fir u-tsri___ Gil-'ad re-khev Mitz-ra-yim sha-lal-ti lakh bat e-lef ha-ze-mer et-leh lakh ma-gen___ min ha-ye-or___ ad___ ha-Yar-den

עֵץ הָרִמּוֹן נָתַן רֵיחוֹ
בֵּין יָם הַמֶּלַח עַד יְרֵחוֹ
שָׁב חוֹמָתִי גְּדוּדֵךְ מִנְּדֹד
שָׁב תַּמָּתִי דּוֹדֵךְ מִדֹּד
אוֹצְרוֹת אוֹפִיר וּצְרִי גִלְעָד
רֶכֶב מִצְרַיִם שָׁלַלְתִּי לָךְ בַּת
אֶלֶף הַזֶּמֶר אֶתְלֶה לָךְ מָגֵן
מִן הַיְאוֹר עַד הַיַּרְדֵּן.

The arrow returns to its bow;
the pomegranate pines for the tree;
so does the soldier yearn for his loved one.

Recipes for a Rosh Hashanah Menu

Date Muffins

3 eggs
½ cup sugar
1 cup chopped nuts
½ cup raisins (soak in
water to plump)
1 10-oz. container dates, chopped

Beat eggs and sugar together. Add rest of ingredients. Spoon into mini muffin holders. Bake at 350° for 15–20 minutes.

Fruit Salad with Pomegranate

Fill a small bowl with pomegranate seeds and place in the center of a large platter. Arrange seasonal fruit around it and decorate with mint leaves. Here are some suggestions:

pineapple, cored and cut into cubes
nectarines, sliced
strawberries, whole or halved
raspberries
green grapes

blueberries
mango, cubed
papaya, cubed
kiwi, sliced

Baked Apples

6 large baking apples
$\frac{1}{3}$ cup granola or other cereal
$\frac{1}{2}$ tsp. cinnamon
$\frac{1}{4}$ tsp. nutmeg
raisins (optional)
walnuts, finely chopped (optional)
2 tsp. orange juice
$\frac{1}{3}$ cup honey
3 Tbsp. margarine, melted
$\frac{3}{4}$ cup apple juice

Core the apples with a knife or an apple corer. Place them in a 9-inch square baking pan. Prepare filling: combine granola, cinnamon, nutmeg, orange juice, and 3 Tbsp. of the honey. Spoon filling into center of each apple. Combine remaining honey with margarine and apple juice. Pour over apples. Bake at 350° for 30 minutes, basting with pan juices, until apples are tender when pierced. Serve warm or cooled.

Apple Maraba (Preserves)

4 slightly tart apples
$\frac{1}{2}$ cup water
$\frac{1}{4}$ cup brown sugar
8 cloves
1 Tbsp. rose water
2–3 drops red food coloring (optional)

Peel and core apples. Cut into quarters. Set aside. Pour water into a deep cooking pot. Add sugar, bring to boil, and simmer until sugar dissolves. Add apples, cloves, rose water, and food coloring. Bring to boil and simmer until apples are soft (about 10 minutes).

Vegetable Cutlets

1 package of frozen mixed vegetables
that includes green beans
2 medium potatoes
2 Tbsp. matzah meal or breadcrumbs
(plus an additional cup for coating)
1 egg
1 tsp. cilantro or parsley, chopped
1 tsp. salt
pepper to taste
oil for frying

Cook vegetables according to package directions. Mash. Wash potatoes well.
Boil, cool, peel (if you wish), and mash. Add to vegetables. Add matzah meal,
egg, and spices. Form into balls and flatten slightly. Put additional crumbs in a
plate. Dip the patties until they are well-coated. Heat oil in frying pan. Fry the
patties until golden. Turn and fry on the other side. Drain on paper towels. Or
bake the cutlets in an oiled pan. Drizzle the tops with oil, bake at 400° for 10
minutes, turn, drizzle with more oil, and bake for another 10 minutes.

Roasted Green Beans Amandine

2 lbs. green beans, ends trimmed
2 Tbsp. extra virgin olive oil
coarse sea salt or kosher salt
toasted slivered almonds

Preheat oven to 500°. Lightly oil a large shallow pan. Arrange the green beans
in a single layer, drizzle oil over them and toss until evenly coated. Roast for
about 15 minutes until the beans are well browned, shaking the pan
occasionally. Transfer to a serving bowl and sprinkle with salt to taste. Add
toasted slivered almonds and serve.

Roasted Pumpkin Seeds

Rinse the fibers from the seeds and place in a baking pan. Toss with melted butter or oil, and brown for 1 to 1-½ hours in a 250° oven. Dry in a warm, airy place.

Pumpkin Bread

3½ cups flour
2 tsp. baking powder
2 tsp. baking soda
½ tsp. salt
⅛ tsp. nutmeg
⅛ tsp. cloves
1 tsp. cinnamon
2⅓ cups sugar
⅔ cup margarine, softened
2 eggs
1 1-lb. can pumpkin
⅔ cup water
chopped walnuts (optional)

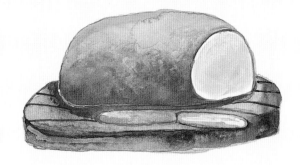

Sift together all dry ingredients except sugar. Set aside. Cream sugar, eggs, and margarine. Add pumpkin and water. Add dry ingredients. Place in two oiled loaf pans. Bake at 350° for 45 minutes–1 hour.

Beetroot Leaves Mahmoosa

½ lb. leaves from a bunch of fresh beets, or ½ lb. spinach
½ cup water
1 garlic clove, finely chopped
1 small piece ginger, finely chopped
1 medium onion, finely chopped
2 Tbsp. oil
¼ tsp. turmeric
½ tsp. salt
2 large eggs, beaten

Remove tough stems from spinach or beet leaves. Chop. Put water and greens into large saucepan and bring to boil. Cook covered, about two minutes. Cool. Drain, squeezing out as much water as possible.

Saute garlic, ginger, and onion in oil until lightly browned. Add turmeric and salt. Keep stirring for about two minutes. Add greens and continue to stir for another two minutes. Add eggs and stir until scrambled.

Beets in Ginger and Honey

3 small beets, peeled
Olive oil

Syrup:
¼ c. water
2 Tbsp. honey
1-inch piece of ginger, peeled and sliced finely
1 Tbsp. lemon juice (optional)

Preheat oven to 400°. Toss beets with olive oil and roast, covered with foil, for 30 minutes. The beets will be sizzling, so turn them carefully and roast for another 30 minutes. Cool and slice. Eat as is or with syrup: Combine water, honey, and ginger in small saucepan. Simmer over low heat for 10 minutes. Add lemon juice if desired. Cool, pour over beets, and marinate in refrigerator for at least 2 hours. Drain liquid before serving. May be served warm, at room temperature, or chilled.

Spinach Salad

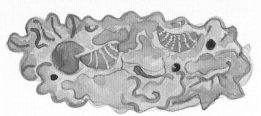

1 lb. spinach
8 oz. mushrooms, sliced
1 avocado, peeled and sliced
1 3-oz. can mandarin oranges, drained
alfalfa sprouts
dried cranberries or fresh pomegranate seeds
roasted cashews

Wash spinach leaves thoroughly to remove any dirt. Pat dry with paper towels. Add mushrooms, avocado, mandarin oranges, and sprouts. Top with dried cranberries and cashews, if desired. Toss with your favorite dressing or use dressing in green salad recipe below.

Roasted Leeks

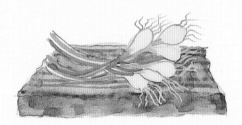

8 leeks
2 Tbsp. olive oil
1 cup vegetable or chicken broth
salt and pepper

Cut off the dark green tops of the leeks and discard. Slice light green and white sections. Put the slices in a bowl of water and swish around until the dirt between the layers settles to the bottom. Remove leeks and drain in colander.

Preheat oven to 425°. Lightly oil a 9×13-inch baking dish. Brush the leeks with oil and arrange in the dish. Roast for 20 minutes. Add the broth and roast for another 10 minutes. Transfer to a serving dish and sprinkle with salt and pepper to taste.

Greens Salad

Lettuce, cleaned and dried
  (use a mixture of mesclun, romaine, red, or green leaf)
cucumbers, peeled and sliced
green olives
scallions or chives, sliced
cherry tomatoes
toasted sunflower seeds
chickpeas
boiled red potatoes, quartered

SALAD DRESSING:
1 Tbsp. olive oil
2 Tbsp. cider vinegar
1 Tbsp. tamari (soy) sauce
1 clove fresh garlic, pressed
$\frac{1}{8}$ tsp. dried ground mustard
$\frac{1}{8}$ tsp. dill
$\frac{1}{8}$ tsp. oregano
a squeeze of fresh lemon

Place all salad ingredients in a bowl. In a separate bowl, whisk together all the dressing ingredients. Pour dressing over the salad and toss.

About the Author and Illustrator

Rahel Musleah is originally from Calcutta, India and traces her family's roots back to seventeenth century Baghdad. She is a Jewish educator, singer, writer, and storyteller, as well as an award-winning journalist. She lives in Great Neck, NY, and has two children.

Judy Jarrett has been illustrating children's books for almost 20 years. She is a self-trained artist who often shows her 3-dimensional work (such as hand-painted furniture) at fairs and galleries. She has one granddaughter and lives in Indianapolis, IN.

English versions of blessings (pages 15, 33, 37, 43) reprinted with permission from the New Year's prayerbook edited and translated by Rabbi David de Sola Pool, published by the Union of Sephardic Congregations, copyright 1954.

"The Magic Pomegranate:" Adaptation reprinted with permission of the publisher, Jason Aronson, Northvale, NJ, from *Jewish Stories One Generation Tells Another*, by Peninnah Schram, copyright 1987,1993.

"The Apple Tree's Discovery:" Reprinted with permission of the publisher, Jason Aronson, Northvale, NJ, from *Chosen Tales: Stories Told by Jewish Storytellers*, edited by Peninnah Schram, copyright 1995.

"Tuli's Treasure:" Inspired by a story told by the Jews of Turkey.

"Two at a Time:" Inspired by a story told by Jews of Tunisia.

"The Proper Place for a Tail:" From *A Treasury of Jewish Folklore*, by Nathan Ausubel, copyright 1948, 1976 by Crown Publishers, Inc. Used by permission of Crown Publishers, a division of Random House, Inc.